ENDORSEMENTS

"Cardboard has never looked so good! In a world that's bombarded with boxes, this gorgeous book from Barbara Rucci couldn't have come at a better time. For anyone with a soft spot for the environment, *Cardboard Creations* is brimming with process-driven art projects that will delight and educate children on how to become resourceful makers."

– Rachelle Doorley, arts educator, author of *Tinkerlab: A Hands-On Guide for Little Inventors*, and founder of the popular creativity blog, *Tinkerlab*

"Bar always has the best ideas and those in *Cardboard Creations* are no exception. What an absolutely beautiful book filled with fun and creative projects that kids will LOVE!"

– Jean Van't Hul, author of *The Artful Parent* and *The Artful Year*, and founder of the family art blog, *The Artful Parent*

"*Cardboard Creations* is an absolute gem for any teacher or parent. The activities are not only resourceful and engaging during the process of creation, but they captivate a child's imagination long after the project is over. Many of the finished pieces can become a costume, a playhouse, a puppet, or a favorite toy. This intersection of art, play, and ingenuity is what creativity is all about!"

– Megan Schiller, teacher and founder of *The Art Pantry*, an online design studio specializing in children's creative play spaces

"*Cardboard Creations* inspires children to connect with a resource that is plentiful and free, in meaningful and personal ways that can make your home and our planet a more beautiful place to live!"

– Jennifer Bryant, arts educator and founder of *Small Hands Big Art*, an art studio in Charlotte, North Carolina

"My philosophy as an author, teacher, mom, and educator has always been to honor the natural creative process children use to explore, discover, experiment, and create with materials and supplies on hand. *Cardboard Creations* offers children a plethora of process art explorations with cardboard and more. Barbara Rucci's art invitations value and inspire the creative process of learning. I'm delighted to offer my highest recommendation of this book as important and valuable for children's natural and precious creativity."

– MaryAnn F. Kohl, educator and award-winning author of over 20 children's art books

"Barbara has given not only beautiful photos that make you want to save every box, paper tube, or jar you can get your hands on, but she also reveals the secret to what captures a child's attention and gets the child to want to take part in a creative process. This book isn't just about making something, it is about constructing, color mixing, designing, and creating at a level that works no matter what age child you have. As a teacher for over 30 years, I can confidently say that Barbara's insightful words at the beginning of the book as well as the easy-to-do ideas she shares will inspire the very best kind of creative thinking and participation at home or in the early childhood classroom!"

– Deborah Stewart, veteran preschool teacher and founder of the popular blog, *Teach Preschool*

Published by
The Innovation Press
1001 Fourth Avenue, Suite 3200
Seattle, WA 98154
www.theinnovationpress.com

Printed by Worzalla.
Production Date: May 2019

10 9 8 7 6 5 4 3 2

Many of the designations used by manufacturers and sellers to distinguish their products are claimed as trademarks. Where those designations appear in this book and The Innovation Press was aware of a trademark claim, the designations have been printed with initial capital letters.

All of the activities in this book are intended to be performed under adult supervision. Appropriate and reasonable caution is recommended when activities call for any objects that could be of risk, such as hot glue, sharp scissors, or small objects that could present a choking hazard. If you are unsure of the safety or age appropriateness of an activity, please contact your child's doctor for guidance. The recommendations in the activities in this book cannot replace common sense and sound judgment. Observe safety and caution at all times. The author and publisher disclaim liability for any damage, mishap, or injury that may occur from engaging in the activities described in this book.

ISBN: 978 1 943147 60 1
Library of Congress Control Number: 2018958239

Typesetting by Kerry Ellis.

CARDBOARD CREATIONS

Open-Ended Exploration with Recycled Materials

Barbara Rucci

CONTENTS

ART PROJECTS

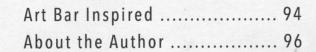

INTRODUCTION

USE IT UP, WEAR IT OUT, MAKE IT DO, OR DO WITHOUT.

- Proverb of unknown origin

Repurposing is a state of mind. I was raised to use what I had, to collect and play with loose parts, to mend and fix broken stuff, and to give new life to my worn-out things. When my children were little, I renewed their torn jeans with monster patches, then turned them into bags when they outgrew them. My husband's old shirts became their art smocks, and I even made quilts from their most beloved clothes.

As an art teacher, I carry the same mind-set. Jam jars become paint jars, egg cartons become paint palettes, and every shoebox is saved for a future dollhouse or puppet theater. There is something so satisfying about setting up an art class without spending any money on new supplies. I actually love the "no-cost" challenge. I scrounge around the house and pull out anything I can find — old sheets, twigs from the kindling box, or yarn trimmings I saved from that time we made pom-poms.

Among everything I collect, nothing is more useful than cardboard. I don't save every box that comes into the house, but almost. I flatten out big pieces and fit the medium and smaller boxes inside of each other, and I keep all of them neatly stacked in the basement. Organization is crucial when you are a collector. I use aesthetically pleasing bins to store recyclables in the art room, and I keep smaller loose parts in jars on shelves. The goal is to balance my saver tendencies with my desire to create a clean living space. With thought and planning, I'm here to tell you that it can be done!

Cardboard Creations is an ode to my love of repurposing, and to the wonders that occur when children reuse objects otherwise headed for the garbage bin. There is definitely a freedom that a child feels when they are given an item to reimagine, rather than facing a blank piece of paper. My philosophy as an art educator, and as a mom, is to set out materials in an inviting way with minimal to no instructions, and just let the children go. In the art teacher world, we call these setups creative invitations. They are child-led explorations of materials. The value lies in the process rather than the finished product.

The best part about creative invitations? As a parent or teacher, you don't need to know much about art or how to draw a straight line in order to build a creative life for your family. It can be daunting sometimes to set up craft projects for children, especially if you don't feel crafty yourself. My projects are not crafts. They are child-led, so no artistic ability on your part is necessary. There are some loose instructions, but as you'll see, they can be broadly interpreted and there is never a right or a wrong way to do something.

Occasionally, I will introduce a new skill, like pulling off pieces of tape, stringing beads, studying the elements of the face, or wrapping yarn around an object. Learning new techniques is exciting for young artists, and soon you will see them using these new skills when exploring their own ideas.

When talking to children about their art, inquire about their process and engage them with thoughtful comments. Rather than saying, "It's great!", which is more of a judgment and does not acknowledge their effort, talk about the design or the color. Ask about how something was made, or how it will be used in the future. Don't worry – at the end of each project, I have included sample ideas on how to engage with children. Taking the time to ask children thoughtful questions and to comment on their work encourages them to share what they are thinking, which makes them feel noticed and builds their creative confidence.

In this book, each activity is a creative invitation. The projects are not about making something pretty, but they are about shaping and preparing young minds to use all of their senses and be open to every possibility they can imagine.

If there is one bit of wisdom I would like to pass on to you about encouraging children's creativity, it is this: Give them a dedicated space, a shelf or two of materials that are organized and accessible, a hefty supply of recyclables, and the freedom to explore their own ideas. That's all they need to spark their imaginations and become the innovators and repurposers of the future!

XO, BAR

COLLECTING RECYCLED MATERIALS

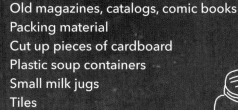

SMALL ITEMS

Bottle tops
Jar lids
Wine corks
Buttons
Nuts, bolts, washers
Laundry scoopers
Ribbons from gifts
Old puzzle pieces
Yogurt cups
Toilet paper rolls
Creamer cartons
Old music CDs
Baby food containers or jars
Packing peanuts

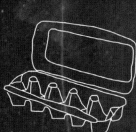

MEDIUM ITEMS

Mismatched socks
Fabric scraps
Plastic berry containers
Green molded pulp berry containers
Glass jars from jam, pickles, sauce
Egg cartons - both plastic and cardboard
Plastic water or juice bottles
Milk cartons
Paper towel rolls
Sticks
Brown paper grocery bags
Newspaper
Telephone directories
Maps
Bubble wrap
Cereal boxes
Tea and cracker boxes
Wood scraps
Used wrapping paper

Old magazines, catalogs, comic books
Packing material
Cut up pieces of cardboard
Plastic soup containers
Small milk jugs
Tiles

LARGE ITEMS

Large milk jugs
Cardboard boxes
Flat cardboard pieces
Pizza boxes
Blueprints
Wire hangers
Coffee cans
Sticks
Bigger wood scraps
Molded packing material for large items
Large food containers, like pickle jars

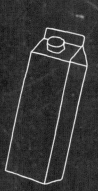

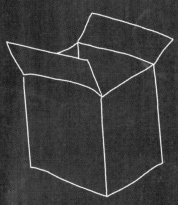

STORING RECYCLABLES

Here are some ways to store your collected materials and stay organized so that your recyclables don't take over your house!

1. I love keeping my recyclables in this lovely canvas laundry basket. I throw anything in that fits, mostly the small and medium sized items on the list. Once the basket is full to the top, I know that it's time for me to stop collecting and start using. My students will rummage through looking for stuff, so things do tend to fall on the floor, but it's easy enough to pick up and put back. I found this basket on Amazon (search for canvas laundry basket or hamper).

2. I am constantly breaking down cardboard boxes and cutting them up into small, medium, and large pieces. I put the small and medium pieces propped sideways in a box. I like getting boxes from the grocery store that have handles cut out on the side. The larger pieces I store sideway; I usually slip them behind a bookcase or a dresser, or lay them on top of other boxes in the basement or attic. My favorite box cutter is the Klever Kutter.

3. I save lots of glass jars and use them to store the small items from the list. I also save coffee cans for sticks or other tall, vertical things. I arrange these jars on a shelf in the art area so that they are easily seen and accessible. I believe that if you store materials so that the kids can see them, they will be more likely to use them! I also love saving the odd little things like these bread ties or old puzzle pieces. You can never have too many jars filled with stuff!

MASTER SUPPLY LIST

These are all of the art supplies you'll need to do every project in this book (not including recycled materials).

PAINTING & DRAWING

Tempera paint

Watercolor paints

Liquid Watercolor paint

Paint brushes

Foam roller

Black permanent marker

Colored markers

PAPER

Watercolor paper

Colored paper

Patterned paper or scrapbook paper

Cut up old art

Newspaper

ADHESIVES

White glue

Glue sticks

Low-temperature glue gun

Tape

Colored tape or washi tape

TOOLS

Scissors

Utility knife

CRAFT SUPPLIES

Craft sticks

Straws

Neon labels

Yarn

Pipe cleaners

Ribbon pieces

Pom-poms

Fabric scraps

Beads (e.g., wooden beads and pony beads)

Cotton swabs (e.g., Q-tips)

Toothpicks

OPTIONAL

Glitter

Cupcake liners

Sequins

Feathers

Neon tempera cakes

Glitter glue

COLOR FAMILIES

Little ones like to mix all the colors together.
To avoid "mud" paintings, set out colors that are in the same family.
You can always add the color white so kids can explore shade and value.
(Avoid putting opposite colors together: purple and yellow, orange and blue, green and red.)

1. yellow, orange, red, pink

2. blue, turquoise, green, yellow

3. pink, purple, periwinkle, blue

4. teal, green, blue, mint

5. peach, pink, purple, magenta

6. magenta, yellow, orange, pink

7. dark blue, light blue, turquoise, periwinkle

8. cream, red, yellow, hot pink

SHOEBOX THEATER

- -

*Redesign a humble shoebox into a colorful theater for stick puppets
to inspire hours of imaginary play.*

MATERIALS

Shoebox
Utility knife
Tempera paint
Paint brush
Glass of water
Damp sponge or paper towel
Colored tape or washi tape
Scissors
String

For stick puppets:

Large craft sticks
Washi tape
Scissors
Black marker
Yarn

PROCESS

Prepare the shoebox for the children by using a utility knife to cut a large window in the front. You can also paint the shoebox ahead of time, using a solid color to cover the outside of the shoebox.

Present the prepared shoebox on a paper-covered table alongside the paint. Repurposed plastic egg cartons make great paint holders.

Paint the top and sides next. Leave the bottom unpainted so the shoebox can stand up to dry.

It is easiest to paint the front of the shoebox first. To make sure the paint colors don't mix and get muddy, encourage children to rinse their brushes in a glass of water and blot them dry in between each color using a damp sponge or paper towel.

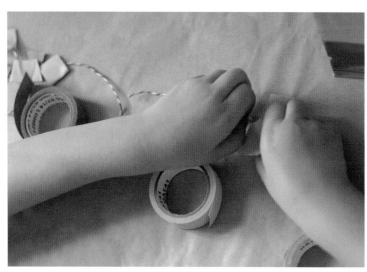

While the shoebox dries, children begin working on decorations, like a mini-garland made of string with pieces of tape wrapped around it.

While the child holds up their finished garland, an adult may need to help tape down the string ends.

Use crafts sticks, tape, yarn, and a marker to create the puppets.

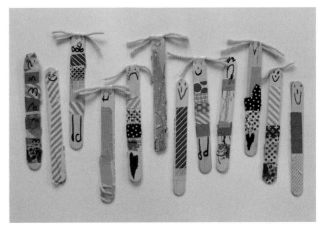

Now it's time to play!

INQUIRE AND ENGAGE

Tell me about your characters.
How do you decide what story to perform?
Will they be singing any songs?

I'm interested to know if *you* like being on stage.
Are your characters wearing costumes?
I can't wait to see the show!

EXTENSIONS

- Write a story with the child and perform it together.
- Create puppet characters from a favorite book.
- Cut animal pictures from magazines and tape them to straws to use as characters.
- Make a curtain for your shoebox theater.
- Create an audience. Make seats and a concession stand.
- Create scenery and attach it to straws to make a movable set design.
- Turn off the lights and shine a flashlight onto the stage.

VARIATIONS

- Use stickers to decorate the shoebox or collage the shoebox using pictures from magazines or other materials.
- Turn the shoebox longways with the opening facing out. Set it inside the lid so the lid extends out to make a stage.
- Create an outdoor amphitheater with several shoeboxes.
- Make a circus-themed theater with clowns and circus animals.

BOX CITY

- - - - - - - - - - - - - - -

Build a city from the ground up in an open-ended project that can be done with one child or a group of children. My art students named their finished structure "The Tower of Teamwork."

MATERIALS

Small to medium cardboard boxes
Utility knife
Low-heat glue gun
Black markers
Colored paper
Scissors
Glue stick
Washi or colored tape
White glue

Neon sticker labels*
Pipe cleaners*
Straws*
Craft sticks*
Chalk markers*

* Optional

PROCESS

Let each child choose a box to create their own unique structure.

Set out a variety of materials to spark ideas for embellishments.

Older children can practice fine motor skills with detail work like creating a clothesline with washi tape and straws.

The children work on their own individual structures before connecting them all with a low-heat glue gun.

Younger children can practice skills like squeezing glue and tearing tape.

Groups of children can work together on other city components such as street signs, a playground, or a garden.

Children can use cupcake liners and craft sticks to create a garden and letter beads to make signs.

An adult can use a utility knife to cut out doors and windows drawn by the children.

INQUIRE AND ENGAGE

Tell me about who lives here.

Remind me how you made that.

How did you decide to stack the boxes that way?

I see that some apartments have more windows. Would you want to live here?

I'm interested to know how people get to their homes.

EXTENSIONS

- Make furniture for your house.

- Make cars and vehicles for the people who live there.

- Make a porch, balcony, staircase, or pool.

- Create characters for your home, such as mice, robots, fairies, gnomes, aliens, superheroes, butterflies, and ants.

- Create a bridge to a secret garden or a tunnel to a night playground.

- Design a lopsided village, patterned houses, a rainbow town, grass roofs, or an art studio.

VARIATIONS

- First put the boxes together and cut out the windows and doors, then let the children paint if you're short on time.

- Design a structure that would work in a windy, sunny, cold, or rainy environment.

- Design a farm city or an outer space city.

- For a minimal effect, spray paint the whole structure white and then let the children paint it. Or for a mess-free version, they can color the white structure with markers and embellish with stickers.

- Use shoeboxes without the lids so that they become open rooms, like a dollhouse.

PAPER BAG COLLAGE MASKS

*Brown paper bags from the grocery store are perfect
for making masks — a classic craft that never loses its magic.*

MATERIALS

Brown paper grocery bags
White glue
Colored paper
Scissors
Black marker*
Small craft pom-poms*
Feathers*
Chalk markers*
Fabric scraps*

Straws*
Ribbon*
Yarn*
Balloons*
Glitter*
Sequins*

* Optional

PROCESS

Prepare the bag first by placing it on the child's head.
Locate their eyes and mouth and outline them on the bag.
Remove the bag and cut eye and mouth hole openings
for the children before they begin.

Children share materials as they work on their masks
independently.

Shaking glitter on top of glue is exciting and enables children to build arm strength.

Children practice gluing materials onto their bag. With younger children, the mask may not look like a face. Just remember that the process is more important than the outcome.

Black marker can be used to add finer details to the mask.

Small balloons add an interesting element and can be attached with white glue or tape.

The finished masks are playful and unique, reflecting each child's personality.

INQUIRE AND ENGAGE

If your mask could talk, what would it say?
Do you feel different when you wear your mask?
I wonder if your mask has special powers.

I noticed you used every color pom-pom.
Is your mask a person or an animal?
Tell me more about this wonderful detail.

EXTENSIONS

- Cut openings for the shoulders so the paper bag rests on the child's head.

- Make a hat or ears on top of the bag.

- Use yarn to make hair.

- Cut toilet paper rolls into small circles and use them for a beard.

- Have the child write a story with friends using their masks.

- Make an impromptu stage in your house for the children to perform in their masks.

VARIATIONS

- Create characters from a storybook.

- Make animals, robots, superheroes, or insects.

- Try a black-and-white version using black paper for collage, white paint, white cotton balls, and any other black or white material.

- Use small paper sacks and make hand puppets instead of masks.

PATCHWORK HOUSES

- -

Children love this mixed-media approach to creating playful houses from cardboard.

MATERIALS

Cardboard
Black marker
White tempera paint
Fabric scraps

Scissors
White glue
Buttons or beads*

* Optional

PROCESS

Prepare the cardboard for the child by cutting it into the shape of a house, then set out the cardboard with a variety of materials.

Children draw with black markers first, then begin to paint.

Buttons or beads can be brought out when the houses are nearing completion. Setting out materials in intervals extends the project and keeps everyone working in unison.

After painting, children glue on the fabric patches. Most children choose to go back and forth between drawing, painting, and gluing.

Squeezing glue is a wonderful hand-strengthening activity. It's also fun!

Children are so proud of their patchwork houses!

Some children may use less white paint. Each artist makes different choices.

Multiple houses can be made to create a village.

INQUIRE AND ENGAGE

Tell me about who lives in your house.
I can see there are lots of windows.
Is there a window for each bedroom?

I noticed that you added buttons for decoration.
Is there a basement?
Would you want to live here?

EXTENSIONS

- Make a stand for your house by cutting slots into two small pieces of cardboard and slipping them on the bottom.

- Create people for your house from craft sticks, corks, or rocks.

- Make an outdoor space that surrounds your house.

- Make multiple houses in different sizes to create a village.

- Design a shop, a grocery store, or a post office.

VARIATIONS

- This project would work just as well with paper collage material. Fabric is not necessary if you don't have any.

- Use all colors of paint rather than just white.

- An adult can cut out windows and doors with a utility knife.

- Use bubble wrap to print "shingles" on the house by painting a piece of bubble wrap and then pressing it onto the house, transferring the paint and creating texture.

MINI-WATERCOLOR QUILTS

Presenting a child with a big piece of cardboard to make a collage is a wonderful opportunity for them to work on design elements such as space, line, shape, color, and balance.

MATERIALS

Watercolor paper cut into small sizes
Liquid Watercolor paint
Cotton swabs (such as Q-tips)
Large piece of cardboard
Glue sticks
Colored tape or washi tape

Scissors*
Chalk markers*
Regular markers*

* Optional

PROCESS

The children begin by painting with cotton swabs, which allow for a variety of strokes and shape-making while honing fine motor skills.

The small format inspires children to create many paintings.

Once the children have made six or more paintings, they can begin working on their quilt.

Use glue to mount the paintings onto the cardboard, then use tape for added flair if desired.

Artists may want to incorporate different shapes into their quilts. Allowing children to have a voice and a choice is what makes process art so valuable.

Using tape is a great fine motor exercise. Children can use their hands to tear pieces or use scissors to cut pieces, depending on their preference.

Arranging smaller shapes together to form a bigger pattern flexes the child's design muscles, and creates a structured yet artful collage.

INQUIRE AND ENGAGE

I noticed that you made lots of different shapes with the cotton swabs.
How many colors did you choose?
Was it difficult to rip (or cut) the tape?

I can see you worked hard arranging your quilt.
Could you make an even bigger quilt?
How many paintings would you need?

EXTENSIONS

- If you are working in a group, connect all the quilts together to make one large collaborative piece.

- Supply colored paper shapes to add to their collage.

- Add in some 3-D collage materials such as buttons, straws, pom-poms, and beads.

- Use fabric squares to embellish the collage.

- Use wire and loose beads to create a beaded hanger for your finished quilt.

VARIATIONS

- Create an underpainting with tempera paint on the cardboard. After it dries, collage the mini-paintings on top for a rich, layered look.

- Children can cut up their mini-artwork with scissors before collaging.

- Make a patchwork quilt.

- Offer different shapes of paper to start, such as triangle pieces.

STYROFOAM SCULPTURES

*Next time you get a package in the mail that has Styrofoam inside, save it!
Children love the sensory experience of sticking toothpicks into this squeaky material.*

MATERIALS

Recycled Styrofoam
Toothpicks (flat toothpicks also
work well)
Beads
Washi tape

Scissors
Low-heat glue gun*

* Optional

PROCESS

Toothpicks, beads, and tape are all that children need to explore the Styrofoam material.

Children begin by sticking washi tape to the Styrofoam.

After adding tape, it's time for the fun part . . . toothpicks! Some children create a pattern while others choose a more random approach.

Sliding beads down the toothpicks is a great fine motor exercise. Some children like to create patterns with the beads.

Some artists take a minimal approach to their design, while others belong to the camp of "more is more."

These activities are all about experimentation. Children may want to start with toothpicks and then do tape, or use the biggest beads they can find! It's *their* choice.

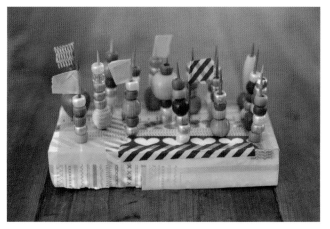

Add tape to the top of the toothpick or an adult can add a bead of hot glue to the top of the toothpick to prevent the beads from falling off.

If you leave this project and supplies out for several days, you may find that your artist comes back and adds to their piece.

INQUIRE AND ENGAGE

What does the Styrofoam feel like?
Is it hard to get the tape to stick?
I see you made a pattern with your beads.

Remind me how you made this part?
Is it difficult to push the toothpicks in?
How many beads did you use?

EXTENSIONS

- Use fabric scraps to create a sail and make the sculpture into a boat.
- Make a person from more than one piece of Styrofoam. Make a robot.
- What would a colorful iceberg look like?
- Set out rubber bands to make a geoboard. Use golf tees for more stability.
- Set out googly eyes to give the sculptures personality.
- Stick and twist pipe cleaners in the Styrofoam to make a roller-coaster.

VARIATIONS

- Use long wooden skewers instead of small toothpicks.
- Cut the Styrofoam into lots of different sizes and build a structure, using toothpicks or skewers to attach them together.
- Paint the Styrofoam first (acrylics work best).
- Find a very large piece of Styrofoam so the whole family can make a collaborative piece.
- Use a dull pencil to poke holes, then glue the beads inside the holes.

BUMPY COLLAGE WALL

----

*Use a variety of recycled materials to create a 3-dimensional collage
that can then be painted with colors children mix themselves.*

MATERIALS

Large piece of cardboard for base

Lots of medium-sized recycled materials

Low-heat glue gun

Tempera paint

Glass jars or plastic containers

Popsicle sticks for mixing

Paint brushes

PROCESS

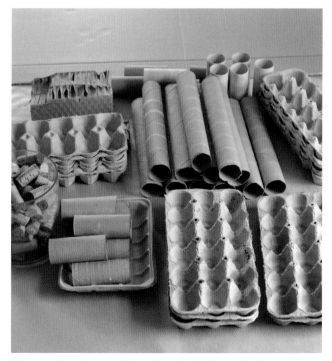

Go on a hunt for a variety of materials (recycled or otherwise) that would be fun to glue and paint.

Mix up the work space by allowing children to work on the floor instead of at a table.

Children can mix their own colors using paints, jars, and popsicle sticks. Rather than offering access to full bottles of paint, control the amount of paint children use by offering only small containers of paint and encouraging children to use spoons to scoop out the paint.

Letting young children use real tools, like a low-heat glue gun, gives them the message that they are trusted, capable builders. Teach them not to touch the tip or the glue and make sure an adult is always closely supervising.

Because young children love to mix all the colors together, set out colors in the same family (see page 11) and white paint. This prevents them from mixing all grays and browns. Older children tend to mix interesting colors on their own.

After paints have been mixed, mount or lean the large piece against the wall so the children can begin to paint. It can also be laid flat on a table or on the floor for painting.

Storing paints in jam jars keeps them fresh in between uses.

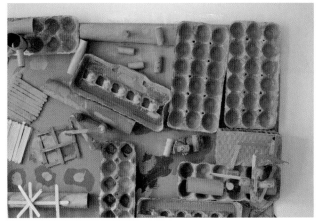

The final piece has a wonderful mixture of muted tones with a few pops of brighter colors – a true collaboration.

INQUIRE AND ENGAGE

How did you mix that color?
Which is your favorite color?
Is it difficult to use a glue gun?

I noticed you were careful with the glue.
How does it feel to paint an egg carton?
I wonder how big you could make this sculpture?

EXTENSIONS

- Add in other recycled collage materials, like paper scraps, buttons, and bottle tops.

- Have the child name the paint colors they've created.

- Set out letter beads and glue down to create words on the collage.

VARIATIONS

- Start by painting all of the pieces first, then glue them together after they've dried.

- An adult can assemble the collage beforehand. This works well for very young children.

- Create an undersea garden, a habitat for mice, or a playground.

- If you have an outdoor space, let the children splatter paint or throw paint-soaked cotton balls on the collage.

WACKY HAIR DAY

Imaginations run wild when given a wacky hair prompt and simple supplies.

MATERIALS

Cardboard	Scissors
Utility knife	White glue
Tempera paint	Yarn scraps*
Jars	Ribbon*
Brushes	Straws*
Yarn	
	* Optional

PROCESS

Cut large, free-flowing cardboard shapes for the children. Once the children have selected their pieces, have them hold up the cardboard just above their nose. Locate their eyes and outline them with a marker, then remove the cardboard and cut out eye hole shapes using a utility knife.

Children begin by adding color to their "hair" with tempera paints.

After painting, children can use glue to attach yarn, ribbons, straws, or other materials.

Encourage your young artist to fill all of the space with paint.

Collect and save yarn bits from pom-pom trimming and other art projects – they are a wonderful, textural addition to collages and mixed-media art.

Some children might want to braid their yarn, which can turn into a braiding lesson. Following the child's lead takes you to all sorts of interesting places.

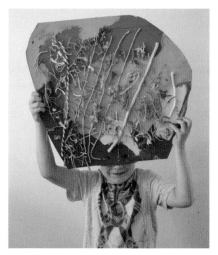

Although there are steps to follow, this project is very open-ended. Each artist presents their own unique story.

INQUIRE AND ENGAGE

Would you ever wear your hair like this?
What is your favorite part?
How did you choose the colors you used?

Remind me again how to braid?
How can you make your own hair crazier?

EXTENSIONS

- Set out some colored paper strips that the children can roll into curls.

- Add pom-poms, feathers, or glitter.

- Make homemade pom-poms, or beads and wire to use as earrings.

- Make ants or bees or another humorous items to add to your hair.

VARIATIONS

- Cut the tops into jagged, spikey, or wavy shapes.

- Use the prompt, "What does your imagination look like?"

- Use collage materials instead of paint, like strips of newspaper and other recycled materials.

- Use paper instead of cardboard and create a crown that fits on top of the child's head.

 Larger pieces of painted cardboard tend to bend. To keep your finished artwork as flat as possible, add a single coat of paint on the back after the front has dried.

TP ROLL SCULPTURES

When you think you are done cutting the cardboard circles, cut more! Children love this simple art invitation and use up the circles very quickly.

MATERIALS

Toilet paper rolls
Utility knife or scissors
Cardboard

White glue
Watercolors

PROCESS

Present each child with a square piece of cardboard to use as a base, a bottle of glue, and a basket of toilet paper rolls cut into circles.

Children love squeezing glue. Remind them at the beginning that "a little dot will do it!"

Building with the circles becomes a quest in engineering and balance.

Wait a day for the sculptures to fully dry. Then set out some paints and let the children explore with color.

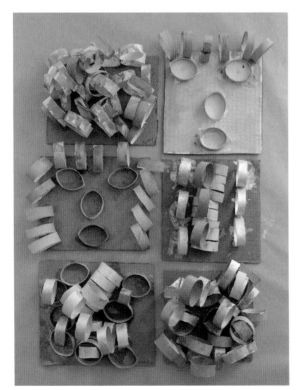

Some children may choose to make faces with their materials. Creativity abounds!

The sculptures can be painted or left plain, whatever your artist prefers. Neon paints highlight the many different directions of the circle shapes.

Haphazard painting gives the structure some texture and weight.

An artist might choose a minimal palette with a pop of bright color inside.

INQUIRE AND ENGAGE

How did you decide to stack the circles that way?

Was it difficult to glue them together?

I can tell that some of them must have been hard to balance.

How tall do you think you could make your sculpture?

It's interesting how you painted the inside of the circles.

If you were magically teeny, would you want to play inside your sculpture?

EXTENSIONS

- Add more collage materials to the sculptures, such as paper scraps and yarn.

- Let the children mix their own colors with tempera paints.

- Make the structure feel like a playground.

- Build a tower.

- Create a perfectly symmetrical sculpture.

VARIATIONS

- Paint the circles first, then glue them together.

- Roll each circle in glue, then add glitter. Dry overnight and then build the sculpture.

- Spray paint the finished sculptures all one color as an homage to the artist Louise Nevelson.

- Make one giant collaborative sculpture with a group, using a bigger cardboard base.

- Use a small cardboard box as the head and use the circles to create a face and hair.

PAPER BAG CROWNS

When brown paper bags are cut open,
they become the perfect length for crowns.

MATERIALS

Brown paper grocery
bags
Scissors
Watercolors
Glass of water
Paintbrush
White glue

Glitter or sequins
Small craft pom-poms

PROCESS

To prepare the crowns, cut down along one side of the paper bag, then cut off the bottom. Flatten it out and cut in half lengthwise. Flatten the creases, then cut zigzags to make the crown top. One bag makes two crowns.

Set out the paints first and bring other materials later. Adding materials as you go can extend the time spent on the project.

Encourage the child to fill in all of the brown space with paint.

Clear the paints from the table and set out the collage materials and glue. Glitter is optional.

Once the crowns are dry (overnight if you use glitter and pom-poms), wrap them around each child's head and tape at the back for a perfect fit.

Children wear their paper bag crowns while making more recycled art!

The brown paper gives the paint colors a lovely, muted tone. For brighter colors, use white shopping bags.

Gluing pom-poms at the top peaks give the crown a true, royal touch.

INQUIRE AND ENGAGE

Why do you think the watercolors look different on the brown paper?

Did any of your paints mix together to make a new color?

How did you decide where to put the pom-poms?

How do you think it would feel to be a queen or king? Would you like to be one?

I wonder what it would be like to rule a kingdom.

EXTENSIONS

- Use scissors and colored paper scraps to collage the crowns.

- Use other collage materials like buttons, straws, and cupcake liners to embellish the crowns.

- Make paper snowflakes to add to the crowns, making them snow queens and kings.

- Use bubble wrap and tempera paints to print some texture onto the crowns.

- Add washi tape to the crowns after they have dried.

VARIATIONS

- Make a fringe at the top of the crown by cutting the tops flat, drawing a line across the middle, and letting the children cut to the middle line, making strips.

- Use white paper shopping bags to achieve more vibrant paint colors.

- For a birthday party, use watercolors and then set out some chalk pastels or oil pastels. That way, you don't have to wait for any glue to dry.

- Make nature crowns using leaves, flowers, and twigs collected in the yard or at a park.

ARTSY PLAYHOUSE

- -

Children will love using foam rollers to paint their houses. Choose colors from the same color family (see page 11) to keep them from getting muddy.

MATERIALS

Large cardboard box
Duct tape
Tempera paint
Paper or plastic plates
Foam rollers or paint brushes
Black marker

Fabric squares*
White glue*

* Optional

PROCESS

Prepare a giant cardboard house out of a big box. Don't cut the door until after it's been painted.

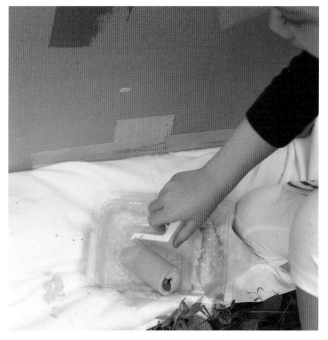

Using foam rollers is a new and different experience for many children. Some foam rollers come in plastic containers that can be used as paint trays. Or you can use paint brushes and plastic or paper plates as paint trays.

Children will want to roll paint on the house all day long – it's *that* fun. Big body movements are great fun and if the weather allows, you can work on the project outdoors.

Once the paint has dried overnight, an adult can cut out the door using a utility knife. Either a child or an adult can then draw windows on the house.

Children might want to begin playing in the house while others work on the roof.

With fabric squares and some glue, children can create a charming patchwork roof.

Transforming an ordinary box into a colorful playhouse creates hours of enjoyment and imaginary play.

INQUIRE AND ENGAGE

What type of structure is this? A townhouse? An apartment? A fort?

Do you think you could live in there?

I'm interested to know how you made all of those different colors.

Can you name all the colors?

I wonder how many people fit inside?

What do you call that type of roof?

EXTENSIONS

- Hang little lights inside and make it a reading nook.

- Continue to patchwork the whole house.

- Use other collage materials to add decoration around the windows, such as pom-poms or buttons.

- Create a garden around the bottom of the house.

- Decorate the inside, such as hanging up paintings, making a rug, and bringing in pillows.

- Make it an art cottage where the children take their art supplies inside and make art.

VARIATIONS

- If you can't get outside and don't want to paint the box inside, skip the paint and use only collage materials, stickers, or markers.

- Make windows that open, with curtains and flower boxes filled with paper flowers.

- Stack a smaller box on top, then another smaller box with a point, and turn it into a rocket ship.

- Cut battlements at the top and turn it into a castle.

- Collect lots of toilet paper rolls and paper towel rolls and glue them on the sides to build a log cabin.

RAINBOW COLLAGE

Start a collection of collage materials by cutting up old art, catalogs, and bits of fabric.
Keep the colors separated and you'll be well prepared for rainbow magic at a moment's notice.

MATERIALS

Cardboard
Utility knife or scissors
Collage materials
Small craft pom-poms
White glue

Hole punch*
Craft wire*

* Optional

PROCESS

An adult can cut a rainbow shape out of cardboard using a utility knife or scissors. If you need more than one rainbow, use the first shape as a template for more rainbows.

Using collage materials sorted by color, children glue down their collage pieces, making design decisions as they go.

Each child approaches their collage differently. This young artist created a patchwork of color.

Pom-poms can be added on top of the collage as an added decoration.

The children pass around different colors to each other as they talk about their rainbows. Making art in a group is very social.

Patterned and textural pieces can come from clothing catalogs and wrapping paper.

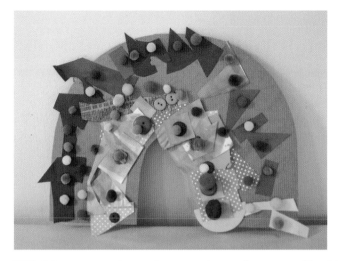 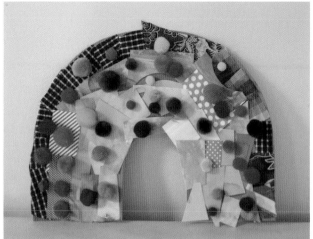

With this process art experience, no two collages are alike. It's also a wonderful way for young children to strengthen their fine motor skills by squeezing glue and manipulating small bits of fabric and paper.

- -

INQUIRE AND ENGAGE

Tell me about all the different colors you used.

Is there a pattern or particular order to your colors?

I wonder how many collage pieces are on your rainbow?

Have you ever seen a rainbow in the sky?
Do you think rainbows are magical?

EXTENSIONS

- Set out washi tape to add to the rainbow.

- Punch two holes at the top and add a wire for hanging. Add beads to the wire hanger for decoration.

- Cut a cardboard cloud shape, collage with white material, and attach to one side of the rainbow.

- Make raindrops and add them to your cloud.

VARIATIONS

- Use paint first, then collage on top.

- Cut out one giant rainbow that can be made with a group.

- Make a 3-D rainbow by attaching two rainbows with a piece of cardboard in between.

- Give the children scissors and larger pieces of colored paper to cut their own collage bits.

- Use flower petals and leaves to make a nature rainbow.

YARN-WRAPPED LETTERS

This colorful and tactile project bridges the gap between process art and craft. Children learn the directed skill of wrapping yarn around an object while simultaneously having the freedom to explore their own design path.

MATERIALS

Cardboard
Utility knife or scissors
Yarn
Masking tape

Washi tape*
Pom-pom makers*

* Optional

PROCESS

Gather yarn, tape, and cardboard. An adult can draw letters on the cardboard and cut them out with a utility knife.

To wrap the letters, pick a yarn color, cut off a long piece (1 to 2 feet), tape the end to the back, then start wrapping. When the child finishes wrapping, they tape the other end to the back. If the child gets tired of wrapping yarn, they can continue decorating their letter with washi tape.

The tape can become part of the design, adding texture and interest.

Younger children tend to wrap quickly. This artist invented her own technique of tucking the yarn underneath when finished.

Cut some pieces of tape and stick them around the edges of a plate. This helps children stay in the flow of wrapping.

Older children tend to spend more time on their letters, making sure the yarn lies flat in neat rows.

Since the yarn is already out, children can make pom-poms to add to their letters. Pom-poms are always a good idea.

INQUIRE AND ENGAGE

How many different colors of yarns did you use?
Is it difficult to wrap the yarn around the letter?
What are *your* initials?

How did you make that pom-pom?
If you could make a whole word, what would it be?

EXTENSIONS

- Set out ribbon bits to weave in between the yarn.
- Make paper flowers to glue onto the letter.
- Punch holes at the top and add a wire hanger. Add beads to decorate the hanger.
- Wrap yarn around a twig, attach the letter to the twig, and hang.
- Create more letters to spell a word.

VARIATIONS

- For younger children, collage the letter instead of wrapping it with yarn.
- Wrap the letter with long strips of fabric scraps.
- Make a letter out of wire for a more transparent look.
- Make a 3-D letter by attaching two identical copies of your letter with a piece of cardboard in between.
- Make cardboard photo frames instead of letters.

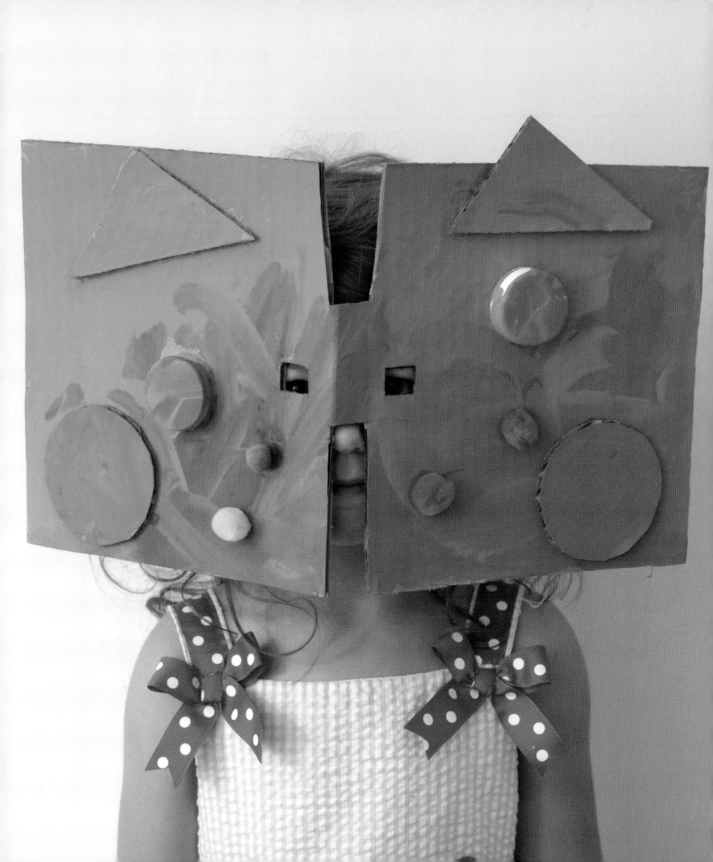

FUNKY EYEWEAR

- -

Inspired by artist and art teacher Neusa López and her carnevale masks, children create fabulous eyewear pieces using basic materials.

MATERIALS

Large piece of cardboard
Small pieces of cardboard
Utility knife
Tempera paint
Recycled bottle tops
White glue

A long, slender strip of cardboard
Masking tape or duct tape
Straws*
Small craft pom-poms*
Feathers*

* Optional

PROCESS

Prepare the eyewear for the children by drawing shapes on the cardboard and cutting them out. Use a utility knife to cut out eye holes after measuring their placement on the child.

The children glue the smaller cardboard shapes and bottle tops to their eyewear. Then they begin painting.

Encourage children to cover all the space with paint.

After they have been painting for a while, set out some other collage materials. Setting out materials at different times helps set the pace and keep the activity going.

Tip: Use a muffin-top pan to hold the paint jars. Children are much more eager to help clean up when they can fit the jars neatly back into place.

To make the eyewear wearable, attach a long strip of cardboard to the back with masking tape or duct tape.

These playful and eclectic pieces challenge young artists to think big and be funky.

INQUIRE AND ENGAGE

I noticed that your work is (or isn't) symmetrical.
How did you decide on those colors?
I wonder how you mixed that color?

Do you wear glasses?
How does it feel to cover your face with this mask?

EXTENSIONS

- Set out sequins or odd-shaped recycled bits like puzzle pieces to add around the edges of the eyewear.

- Collect leaves, flowers, and twigs to add to their eyewear.

- Write a play with the children to act out with their eyewear.

- Take a photo of each child looking up, down, or sideways. Make a photo collage *Brady Bunch* style.

VARIATIONS

- If you don't have access to larger pieces of cardboard, cut out smaller versions of the eyewear and attach a stick to the side so the children can hold them up to their eyes.

- Give the child a creative prompt, such as making eyewear with an animal theme, robot theme, monster theme, or superhero theme.

- Cut out the eye holes so they are bigger, then cover with transparency film to make lenses.

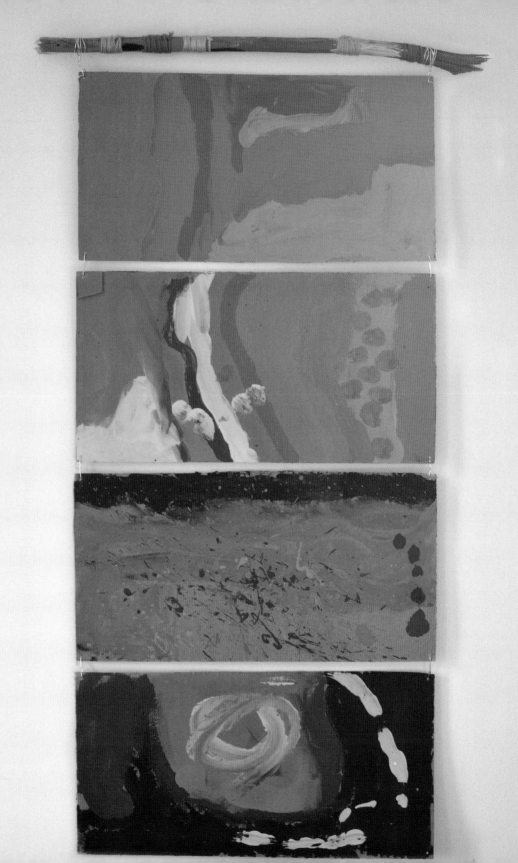

MUSICAL CHAIRS PAINTING

This action art is superb for busy little bodies that like to move.
It's also a great way to practice listening skills and group cooperation.

MATERIALS

Large cardboard panels
Tempera paint
Brushes

Stick*
Yarn*
Hole punch*
Craft wire*

* Optional

PROCESS

Place cardboard and paints around a table. When the music plays, the children paint. When the music stops, they move over to their neighbor's painting.

Music and painting are a joyful combination. These girls are waiting for the music to begin again.

When the music starts again, the children resume painting. The game keeps going until they've made it all the way around the table.

Moving around from one painting to the next creates good energy, and teaches the young artists to encourage each other and try new techniques.

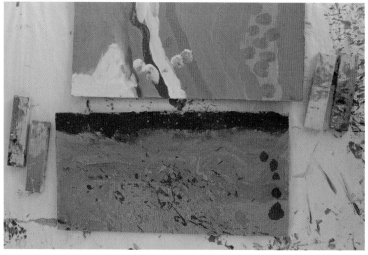

After one round is complete, the children can start another. Some young artists might decide to use wooden blocks to splatter paint.

In the end, all the panels have a unique patina, created from many rounds of musical painting. The blocks are quite beautiful, too.

To make a wall hanging from the final pieces, punch holes in all the corners (except the bottom corners of the bottom piece). Use a pliable craft wire to attach all of the pieces together.

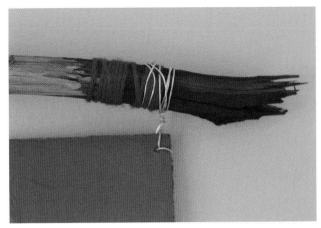

Paint and decorate a stick. Tie the artwork to the stick with more wire. Hang on two small nails.

INQUIRE AND ENGAGE

How does it feel when the music stops?

How did you choose your colors when you got to the next painting?

Did you like painting five different paintings?

Splattering paint looks like fun!

Remind me how the game works?

In the end did you like one painting the best?

EXTENSIONS

- Add a new technique with each round, like splatter paint, printing with potato stamps or bubble wrap, or gluing on collage materials.

- After the paintings dry, draw on top with chalk pastels.

- Create a sculpture on top with cardboard tubes, seeing how tall they can build in one round.

PRO TIP Larger pieces of painted cardboard tend to bend. To keep your finished artwork as flat as possible, add a single coat of paint on the back after the front has dried.

VARIATIONS

- Use toes to hold the paintbrush instead of hands.

- Play musical chairs while making watercolor paintings, collages, or portraits, or while building sculptures.

- Cut out cardboard letters that spell a word or someone's name. This would be a great idea for a birthday party.

- Cut the cardboard into rainbow shapes, star shapes, robot shapes, or animal shapes.

- Cut out face shapes and smaller cardboard pieces to use as facial features. Glue on features in the first round, paint in the second round, and add yarn hair and other details in the third round.

GIANT DONUTS

Creating cardboard sweets is pure fantasy and joy. These donuts make the best photo-ops with little faces popping through.

MATERIALS

Cardboard
Scissors or utility knife
Tempera paint
Ribbons

Straws
Cupcake liners
White glue

PROCESS

An adult can freehand draw and cut out donut shapes. Misshapen circles often create more authentic and charming donuts.

Cut the cupcake liners into strips and cut the straws into smaller pieces. Other materials can also be used for the toppings. Collect all topping materials into trays for later use.

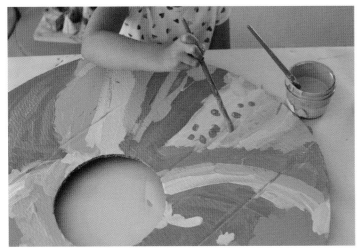

The children begin by painting their donuts. Adding a little white when mixing colors lightens the colors and makes them more opaque so they can be layered and still vibrant.

Set out the collage materials after the children finish painting.

Encourage the child to place the collage bits carefully. This will extend the project and ensure that the pieces are glued on securely.

Although children will borrow ideas from each other, they stay true to their own unique styles and instincts.

Here are more cardboard sweets that you could try! Use oil pastels for less mess and easier cleanup.

INQUIRE AND ENGAGE

Your donut is very colorful.
What does it taste like?
Do you think you could bake a donut this big?

I see you can put your face right in the donut hole!
What is your favorite type of donut?
I wonder if the sprinkles are different flavors?

EXTENSIONS

- Put some brown paint in a small squeeze bottle and let the children drizzle "chocolate" on their donut.

- Set out other collage materials like pom-poms, sequins, and buttons.

- Press bubble wrap onto the wet paint to create some texture.

- Scrunch up tissue paper into balls to glue onto the donut (this is great for strengthening hand muscles!).

- Take the donuts outside and splatter paint.

VARIATIONS

- Cut smaller donuts from watercolor paper and use watercolor paints for a quicker art project.

- Turn your smaller donuts into a party garland.

- Create puffy donuts by stapling two paper donuts together and then stuffing the inside with tissue. Then paint both sides and hang your creation from the ceiling.

> **PRO TIP** Larger pieces of painted cardboard tend to bend. To keep your finished artwork as flat as possible, add a single coat of paint on the back after the front has dried.

RIBBON WEAVINGS

- -

*Turn a small piece of cardboard into a weaving loom
and teach children about this ancient, artisanal craft.*

MATERIALS

Small piece of cardboard
Scissors
Yarn
Masking tape
Ribbon
Washi tape

Paper strips*
Feathers*
Hole punch*
Beads*

* Optional

PROCESS

Prepare the ribbon weavings for the children by making looms. Cut a piece of cardboard into a rectangle approximately 8 inches by 6 inches. Using a ruler, find the center of the top and bottom, then mark the center and make cuts a half-inch deep in half-inch increments, leaving a one-inch margin on both sides. Add yarn for the warp – the stationery threads running top to bottom – and tape them to the back.

Cut the ribbon into pieces the same width as the loom. If you have some old paintings made on heavier paper, cut them into strips too.

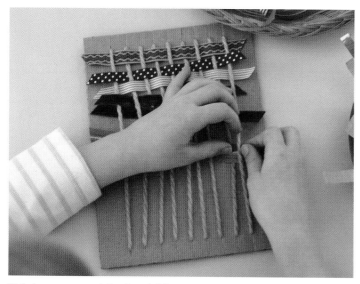

This is a great activity for children to practice the over-and-under technique. Each new row (called the weft) goes in the opposite over-and-under pattern as the row before.

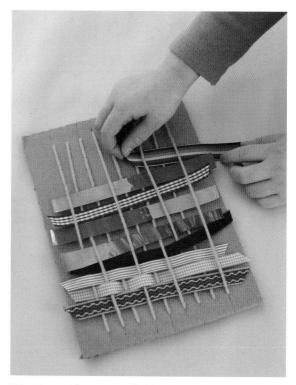

Weaving with pieces of ribbon and paper is very forgiving, so even if the child forgets to change the over-and-under direction with each new piece, that's okay.

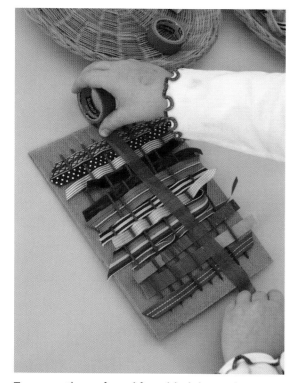

To secure the weft, and for added decoration, set out some washi tape.

To make a hanger, punch two holes at the top corners and tie a piece of yarn to one side. Children can then bead the hanger. Tie to the other side to secure.

Children are calm and quiet as they engage in this relaxing, tactile weaving experience.

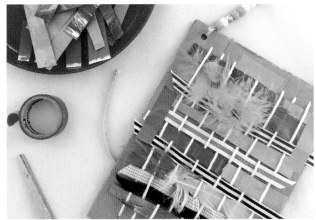

Adding feathers creates more texture and makes the weavings pop.

INQUIRE AND ENGAGE

I noticed you made a pattern with your colors.
How did you decide where to put the tape?
Is it difficult to weave?

Tell me about the process.
Remind me which one is the warp and which is the weft?
I wonder where you will hang your weaving?

EXTENSIONS

- Try using other materials to weave with, like felt shapes, painted newspaper, and maps cut into strips.

- Punch holes in the loom and "sew" yarn or wire throughout the weaving.

- Make a nature weaving using flower stems, leaves, grass, and twigs.

- Glue pom-poms on top for more color and texture.

- Make homemade pom-poms or tassels to hang on the side of the weaving.

VARIATIONS

- Paint the cardboard loom first, then weave on top.

- Make one large cardboard loom and create a collaborative weaving.

- Create a painting, let it dry, cut it into strips, then use the strips to weave the painting back together.

- Use yarn to weave a more traditional weaving.

- Make a rainbow with your weaving.

FAIRY HOUSES

- -

*Small creamer cartons are transformed into little fairy houses
and paper plates become a just-right surface for fairy gardens.*

MATERIALS

Small milk or creamer carton
Sturdy paper plate
Natural materials
Paper scraps cut into strips
Scissors
White glue

Feathers*
Wooden peg doll*
Markers*
Washi tape*
Black marker*

* Optional

PROCESS

Prepare the fairy houses for the children by first cutting
an arched door and then gluing each carton to an upside
down plate. Spray painting is optional.

Go out in your yard, to a park, or on a hike to collect
natural materials.

Once back inside, children can glue the materials onto their houses.

Some children create beds inside their fairy houses.

This artist made a mailbox and a cooking pot for the inside of her fairy house.

Wooden pegs make perfect fairies. If you don't have pegs, wooden craft sticks cut in half also work well.

"Helicopter" seeds from maple trees make perfect fairy wings.

You can use natural materials for the grass, but fabric and paper scraps work too.

INQUIRE AND ENGAGE

Tell me about your fairy's home.
Would you want to live here?
What is your fairy's name?

Where does your fairy sleep?
Who are your fairy's friends?

EXTENSIONS

- Make a laundry line with yarn and washi tape.

- Glue craft sticks to the outside to make it feel more like a cabin.

- Set out colored paper to make paper flowers for the garden.

- Use letter beads to make signs or a name for the house.

- With a low-heat glue gun (supervised by an adult), glue stones to the side of the house, or make a stone wall or path.

- Make a ladder up to the roof, or make a fairy car, or make furniture for inside the house.

VARIATIONS

- If you don't have access to a park or yard to collect natural materials, use other collage materials like straws, buttons, pom-poms, yarn, fabric scraps, pieces of paper, and glitter.

- Let the children paint their fairy houses first with an earthy palette of greens, browns, and golds, or a more colorful palette if you decide to use non-natural materials.

- Turn the plate right side up and fill it with dirt for a sensory play experience.

CARDBOARD ANIMALS

- -

*A box of cardboard scraps and a simple prompt is all that
is needed to spark a child's imagination and lead them to create these charming pets.*

MATERIALS

Small and medium cardboard
pieces

Scissors

Low-heat glue gun

Black marker

Tempera paint

Brushes

PROCESS

Set out the small and medium cardboard scraps and let
the children choose a larger body piece, then smaller
pieces for the head, ears, legs, and tail.

Younger children can instruct an adult on how to glue the
pieces together. Older children may prefer to use a low-
heat glue gun themselves, with adult supervision.

Once the animal structure has been glued together, it's time to paint!

Creativity and play is a child's work. Here they are sharing paints and ideas.

Some children add detail with a black marker.

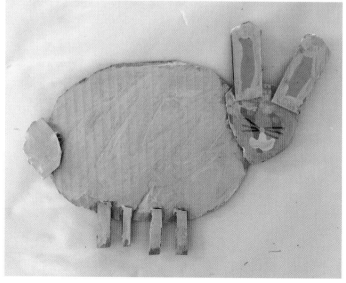

This artist used gold tempera paint to make the bunny feel special.

A striped body and yellow ears are design elements that work well together.

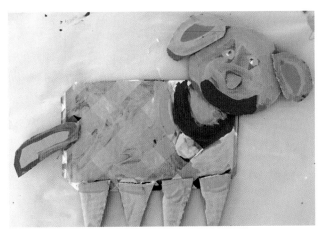

The more children are exposed to open-ended creativity, the more they will intuitively make good design choices. Here the artist uses green as accents in just the right places.

INQUIRE AND ENGAGE

Does your animal have a name?
How did you decide to make that animal?
Do you have any pets?

How did you choose those colors?
Where does your animal live?

EXTENSIONS

- Add collage materials, such as pom-poms, buttons, cupcake liners, and paper scraps.

- Set out yarn and braid collars for their pets.

- Use fabric and scissors to make clothes for the animals.

- Make animal homes or beds using more cardboard.

- Give children an engineering challenge: can they design a cardboard support that enables the animal to stand on its own?

VARIATIONS

- Create "imaginary" animals and encourage the children to make up names for them.

- Make monsters, robots, birds, insects, and aliens.

- Cut round pieces of cardboard and supply lots of smaller bits of cardboard to make faces.

- Go big, making large-scale safari animals such as giraffes, elephants, and lions.

- Make a large underwater animal like a whale or octopus.

IMAGINATION BOXES

- -

Time to clean out the recycle bin? Make an imagination box!
Fill up an empty box with a variety of items and let children create without limitations.

MATERIALS

The contents of an imagination box are completely up to you.
These boxes contain everything from berry containers and
bottle tops to pine cones and buttons. You will also need:

Scissors
White glue
Tape
Low-heat glue gun*

* Optional

PROCESS

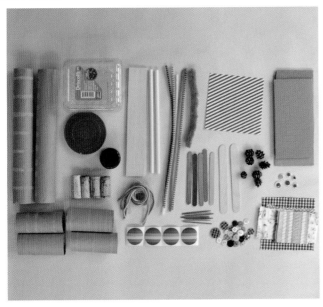

Try to fill up your box with a combination of materials that
represent different sizes, textures, and colors.

Adults can preassemble identical boxes of materials
before children arrive.

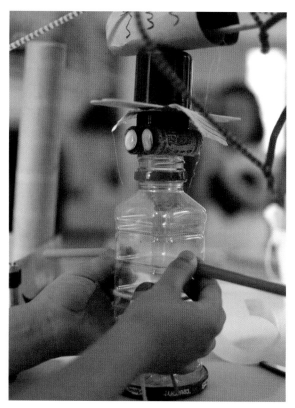

When working vertically, white glue may not be strong enough. Have a low-heat glue gun handy just in case, for use only with adult supervision.

Some children like to work on the floor. Let them spread out if they need to – it's all part of the creative process.

When children are left to explore and experiment with no boundaries, they begin to make bold choices and try new ideas.

This young artist made a house on stilts, complete with a shower curtain.

This child's goal was to use everything in her box. Mission accomplished!

INQUIRE AND ENGAGE

Tell me about your structure.
How did you come up with that idea?
Was it difficult to decide what to do?

What part did you do first?
Is there anything you would change?

EXTENSIONS

- Set out paint when the children are done building their structures.

- Have the children mix their own paint colors.

- Tell the children they have to use everything in the box.

- Ask the children to name their structure or invention.

- Have the children write a poem or a story about their work.

- Set up a museum with all of the finished pieces.

VARIATIONS

- Let children assemble their own imagination boxes.

- Pair children with partners or place in small groups and have them build something together.

- Begin with a creative prompt, for example: Inventions, Best Friend, Flying Machine, Playgrounds, I Live Here.

DIY TABLETOP EASEL

Make a simple table easel from cardboard that folds and stores away.

MATERIALS

Large cardboard box
Duct tape

Utility knife or scissors
Sticky-back Velcro

INSTRUCTIONS

1. Cut the top and bottom flaps off a large box (my boxes were 18 inches by 18 inches by 16 inches), then cut down two sides so that you have two hinged pieces. Each box makes two easels.

2. Cut a long piece of duct tape, about 26 inches long. Attach one end to the bottom right of a cardboard flap. Lift up the tape, find the middle, and fold the tape over in half, taping it back onto itself and the cardboard on the other side to create a strap. Repeat for the left side.

3. Cut a square of sticky Velcro. Attach one side to the duct tape and the other side to the cardboard as a strap fastener. Now you are done!

You may need to weigh the easel down if it wobbles when the child is painting. Taping the easel to the table with masking tape also works to stabilize it.

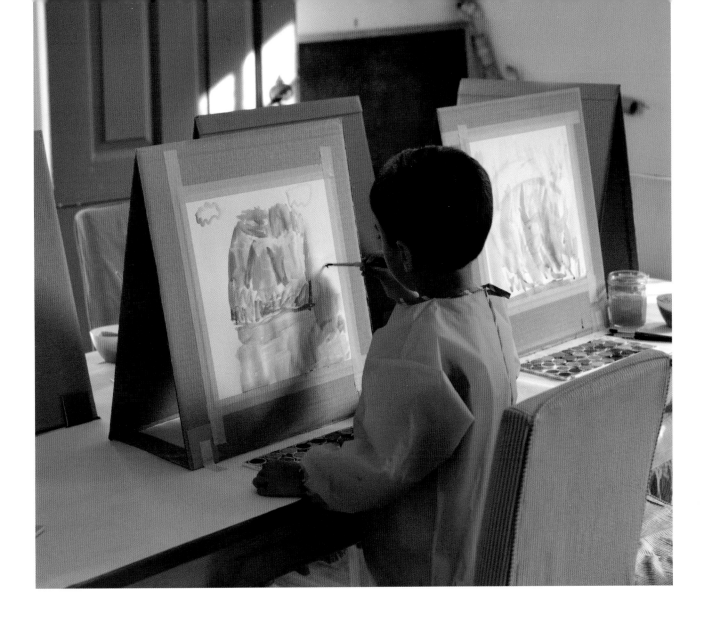

SUGGESTED USES

- Tape large watercolor paper or regular paper neatly to the easel on all edges with painter's tape. After the painting is dry, peel the tape off and you will have a crisp white border.

- Place sticky contact paper on the easel sticky side out and secure the edges with tape or binder clips. Supply the child with collage materials to stick on the contact paper. When they are finished, seal the collage with another piece of contact paper.

- Attach tin foil with tape or binder clips, then let the child paint with tempera paints.

ART BAR INSPIRED

Friends on Instagram share their children's
cardboard creations inspired by my blog, Art Bar.
Join in by tagging @artbarblog and by
using the hashtag #artbarinspired!

yay for cardboard!

xo, Bar

@purpletwig

@thecurious1plus1

@hatchartstudio

@littleloftstudios

@momma_teaching

@julialinsteadt

@teachmakecreate

@collagecollage

@ellachattanooga

@studiosprout

@artseeds.ie

@kimbeehive

@creatingcreatives

@handmakery

@mimosa_montessori

ABOUT THE AUTHOR

My family has called me Bar ever since I was a baby. The name of my blog, Art Bar, is really the perfect description of who I am. I've always been passionate about making things. When I was little, I used to sew clothes for my dolls, and I loved coloring. My passion for fabric and color have stayed with me my whole life. I studied textile design in college and went on to create a children's clothing line. I also dabbled in interior design and quilting before finally choosing graphic design as my career. I was fortunate to be able to work from home, fitting in design projects during nap time, on the weekends, and everywhere in between. In 2012, when my oldest was eleven, I started my blog. At first it was just a journal for my children. Eventually, it became more than just a labor of love, and I found myself teaching art classes in my living room and writing books. My first book, *Art Workshop for Children*, was published by Quarto in 2016. I live with my husband and three children in Connecticut, where a river runs through our yard and maple trees sway overhead.

YOU CAN FIND ME HERE

Blog . . . . artbarblog.com
Facebook . . . . Art Bar
Instagram . . . . @artbarblog
and also . . . . @100daysofArtBar

© Alix Martinez Photography